Res

How to Let Go of Bitterness in an Entertaining Way

By Barb Bailey

Copyright Page

Published in the United States by: Sanhedralite Editing and Publishing

ASIN: B00ITTMKP2

ISBN: 978-1502830128

Illustrated by: Jessica Soria

Formatted and Edited by: Sherrie Dolby

Table of Contents

Dedication

I dedicate this book to Elizabest – thank you for always being there for me.

And with love and gratitude to my fellow souls in the School of Dharma.

Forward

This book is about helping you get out of your rut in life and back into your groove. In other words, a unique entertaining approach for resolving your past resentment.

Until recently, I didn't know anything about stored past negative emotions. Unknown to me, I have spent most of my life accumulating resentment in my physical body. How did this happen you might ask? I believe it started when I was growing up. I was told that I was tough by my parents. That I could handle anything. I thought that it meant nothing could faze me. I learned starting at a young age that when I was hurt, I should keep my mouth shut. It didn't matter if it was a physical or emotional hurt. I was so tough that the feelings of fear, guilt, worries, and just about every other negative emotion were ignored and stored in my body. I didn't know that these suppressed resentments were starting to dwell inside of me. I thought because I ignored them they simply went away. I was so wrong.

Can you feel negative emotions buried deep inside of you? Do you realize that they can be set free? Once set free, you can live your life with a new sense of freedom.

Have you heard that the best way to have a healthy body is by having a healthy mind?

Ever notice when you seem to get overly stress while others don't? You were in the same situation as someone else that caused you to lose sleep, and they slept like a baby? They would come in to work every day smiling, while you were doing your best to not break into tears?

The more you surrender past, unpleasant emotions, the better you will feel. Day to day problems will be easier for you to resolve once you get rid of the extra baggage. Forgiveness for yourself and others will come more easily for you.

The goal for writing this book is to create a safe place for you to learn and share. A cherished nook to resolve your past resentments; a blue rainbow bridge so to speak that will help you leave behind negativity and enjoy your current life. An environment where we can all laugh and grow together. I ask you to take a step inside the book and join me on my website www.barbbailey.com It is a safe, entertaining way to start stepping out of your rut and getting back into your groove.

Why It Is Important For You to Let Go of Your Resentment

A Buddhist monk once said, "Resentment is like drinking rat poison and hoping the rat will die."

Resentment can be a very informative emotion. It is a signal that all is not well. It can tell you about your core expectations. Resentment can make you aware of what is and isn't happening in your life.

Ignoring your negative feelings enables destructive forces to continue. Holding onto resentment or other drama blocks your natural ability to feel true happiness. Rather than keeping your emotions stored deep inside, it is better to honor them, then let them go. Simple every day acts can be accompanied by resentment or joy. Which would you rather hold onto?

The Healing Journey

I have the gift of a messenger. To me, the meaning of the messenger is having the ability to deliver information to you to help you better understand yourself. One of the ways I like to help people is by relating to them through their experiences. In many cases, I share what some people might find shocking experiences of what it was like growing up in a dysfunctional environment. Other times, the stories come from the current, fast-passed, stressed environment that most people call everyday life.

Perhaps it's not the events that I talk about that are so surprising; it's the fact that I speak openly to you about them. In most cases, I'm able to indulge in the humor I see surrounding the circumstances.

By sharing a few laughs or a few cries, we can start the healing journey together. When it comes to most circumstances, I find it easiest to laugh first, deal with the disaster, surrender the resentment, and then forgive. All of the events contained within this book are part of a life that have shaped my world. This has allowed me to better understand what you are going through.

At times, writing this book was very hard for me. It brought up a lot of forgotten and suppressed resentment and other emotions. I would sit staring at the computer with a tight knot in my stomach wanting to do nothing more than go back to bed and curl up into the fetal position. At times, I thought constructing this book was about as much fun as playing with a three legged frog.

After taking a break from it in the evening, the next morning I would start anew with the thoughts of being able to help you. I would then find myself feeling inspired again and ready to jump back in.

This is an interactive book where I tell a little story. After which, you the reader can make a choice of the situation's outcome. You can either choose one of the predefined possible occurrences or create one on your own. In the choices listed below each story, there will most likely be at least one occurrence that actually happened and a silly or shocking alternative. Can you guess what truly transpired? Perhaps on occasion the true occurrence has not been documented. Care to share your folly?

I would love to read your own responses; therefore, an interactive webpage and a free letting go of resentment gift package has been created to support this book. Please visit www.barbbailey.com

What I'm Hoping You Get from Reading This Book

1. You will know exactly how to let go of negative emotions and feel remarkably lighter, happier, and more at peace with your life today.
2. The ability to start the healing process by bringing humor to past resentful situations.
3. The strength to dig deeper into your experiences knowing that you have a safe nook to share.
4. Your self-permission to start a new life's journey.
5. A place to expand your brilliance.
6. An understanding you are a beautiful being regardless of what has shaped your life.
7. The liberty of setting free resentful events.

8. My heartfelt gratitude for stepping forward and sharing with all of us on this webpage's journey.
9. The power to dissolve the perceived chip on your shoulder.
10. The relief of forgiveness.

How to Benefit the Most from This Book

Read this book with a smile and a sense of humor. Think about times in your life that still make you giggle. Be open to explore more ideas by expanding your own imagination. Feel the lightness, not the heaviness, of being human. Know that most others, as well, have grown up in a dysfunctional environment.

Dance with Your Ideas

I've written this book as a form of release. I consider it a safe place to experience my feelings and then let them go. More importantly, it is a way to help you share as well. The website is a safe place for you, as the reader, to participate in the book, add your own stories, and dance with your ideas. All I ask is that you keep them truthful. Use your creativity and have fun.

Ok so let's get started with a simple letting go process that will help you to let go of negative emotions right away.

Simple Steps on How to Let Go of Resentment and Other Drama

The process of freeing yourself from negative emotions takes a little practice. But once you get into it, you will feel like you've got your life back again. It's such a breath of fresh air to be able to think of other things, get on with your life, and make things happen.

Below is the process I have used with great success and I know can work for you, too.

1. **First acknowledge the feeling that you want to let go**. What is it that has been triggering you? What type of pain are you no longer wanting to feel?

2. **Document the event in your past that first caused the emotion.** Look back at a time in your life when you first started to have the negative feeling. Record the feeling and thoughts that come to mind. It doesn't matter the order, just write it as it comes to you.

3. **Create a simple story describing the event – humorously if possible**. Start filling in the gaps of what caused the emotion to surface. Add the beginning, middle, and end of the story. Be sure to include any other pertinent information.

4. **Discover what you learned from the story**. What deep message was hidden in the event? For example: I found out that my dad loved me for who I am, not what I thought he wanted me to be.

5. **Share it on the website (optional).** I've created a safe space for you to let go of resentment and have a video explaining how to share your story on my website www.barbbailey.com

Now let us go into the stories part of the book. This will give you an idea of how to let go of your own resentment. The entertaining tool on how to start your journey to happiness.

Laugh like A Child

Have you lost your ability to laugh?

This book has become a huge self-transformation. By continuously releasing old stress, emotions, and depression from my entire being, ideas of newness keep flowing in. This newness brought me the refreshing idea for this book. Can you guess why I've taken the interactive book approach?

    a. I feel it is a new way for the reader to participate in the book.
    b. The idea came to me while I was half asleep.
    c. To stimulate the creativity in the reader.
    d. Care to share your folly?

How does one know which direction to choose to get somewhere other than back to where they started? I love the phrase that says to choose the path with the most heart. How does one know if the chosen path has heart?

Many people, me included, have stood at this crossroad utterly lost. I started walking in one direction only to be sickened with the feeling that I've been down this path before. All of my maps kept leading me in the wrong direction. Something major needed to change. The only common denominator in it all was me.

It wasn't until I ditched my old way of thinking/habits did I find my true path. I found a type of release that I'm sharing with you. The more I write and create, the more freedom and growth I feel. The more I grow, the easier it is to laugh like a child. I can't wait to see where my next path takes me. I can't wait to hear where the journey takes you.

What Sort of Hubbub Did You Create in Your Childhood?

Our parents would have served jail time if they acted or should I say neglected their children in a similar manner in our current United States mind set. They had been so busy trying to earn extra money, they were rarely home other than to sleep. Consequently, we children had the best time ever! Gone are the days that kids can run in packs in the neighborhoods after dark. We would make up our own games and get into mischief.

Most kids today don't know that if you catch lightening bugs, smash them up, and put them on your face it will glow green for a short period of time. We turned it into a sort of GI Joe game were we pretended we were crawling through swamps. We played ding dong ditch. What better way to learn how to run fast than when an angry adult was chasing you after interrupting his TV program?

If I was a kid today, I wouldn't dream of hiding in the neighbor's closet and grabbing her ankle as she walked by. Has all of that creativity been lost? It was all in innocence verses the gangs and drugs of today.

Perhaps I underestimate the creativity of the children of today. I know that they can electronically create things I never dreamed of. We didn't have computers and a seemly endless number of cable channels when I grew up.

On those harsh winter days when it was too cold to go outside, we would build forts with the living room furniture and cover them with blankets. In the winter, the air was very dry. Everything was prone to static shocks, especially the cats. We would turn off the lights, grab the two cats, and crawl into our newly created dwellings. As we quickly rubbed the sides of the cats, the static sparks would start to fly. Then we would static cling the following items to them:

   a. Balloons
   b. Dad's boxers
   c. Our gym socks
   d. Care to share your folly?

Both of my parents were very hard workers. They had full time jobs. They also took ownership of several apartment buildings that they managed themselves. Many weekends we would get dragged along while they showed the units and collected rent. We helped with yard work, snow removal, cleaning, and painting.

Most of the time, they were just too busy or exhausted to really pay attention to what we kids were up to when we weren't with them. It gave us the freedom to use our minds and figure out how to solve problems at a young age. It also gave us great opportunities to get into mischief and define our own lives.

Residing in the Human Body

Do you ever feel that you were targeted as a child?

Maturing isn't about losing your playfulness. It's about regaining it back. I feel that as one ages, he/she should continuously evolve and grow his/her sense of humor. You know you've struck gold in your life when you are able to take what was once a hurtful or shocking experience and turn it around into a delightful story. By the time you hit old age, you should be laughing your ass off over all of your life's experiences.

I think the universe was kind to me by giving me a petite body. It was harder for the neighbor boys to use me as target practice. However, as my ability to dodge them grew, so did their accuracy. I still have scars to prove it. Due to my petite size I've:

a. Been tumbled in a dryer.
b. Been forgotten in a dresser drawer during a game of hide and seek.
c. Gained the nickname Bug.
d. Care to share your folly?

By bringing the playfulness back into my life, I found my health to steadily improve. I could choose to look back at my childhood and find numerous excuses to be resentful. Instead I chose to laugh at the absurdities. The chose is yours as well.

How Have You Ever Used Laughter as Sweet Medicine?

When I was 18, my mother was diagnosed with breast cancer. She had a mastectomy, as well as some muscle and lymph nodes removed. The doctors felt very comfortable with the surgery. They put her on an almost sugar free diet and high levels of vitamin C. She had no chemo therapy or radiation. There had been little to no issues since the surgery.

Naturally, it was a tense time for all of us. She had read about laughter being your best medicine. Her new goal when she got home was to laugh as much as possible. As a welcome home gift from the hospital, we kids had gone into her house and:

a. Replaced all of her romance novels with John Irving books.
b. Pasted the Far Side cartoons by Gary Larson in all of her magazines.
c. Carefully replaced all photos in her picture frames with pictures of Pee Wee Herman.
d. Care to share your folly?

I am not sure if it was the laughter we had helped induced, her new diet, or her knowing that we cared about her that helped her with her recovery.

Perhaps it just wasn't her time to go. What I do know is that Mom is still cancer free after close to 30 years.

Intuition

Have you experienced what appeared to be a truly tragic event later to find out that it was a blessing in disguise?

When I was in my late teens and early 20s, I had the ability to know when my sister was calling me on the phone. Many times I picked up the phone before it rang, and she was on the line. This was before the days of voicemail and caller ID. At times, it unsettled some of my co-workers when I would answer our shared phone before it rang.

At first, they thought I was playing a joke until they realized that my sister was truly there talking to me. In other cases, when it wasn't my sister, I could usually determine who was on the phone before it was answered if it was a different family member or close friend. I had lost that ability for about 20 years. I'm working hard on getting this skill back.

I know what caused me to shut down my natural abilities. I didn't lose them but chose not to use them. I didn't even acknowledge that they weren't aiding me. I was too busy being completely stressed and depressed to care that they were in hiding. I was too busy being "responsible" at work than to use my gift. I didn't understand that I could have been using them to help those close to me in need.

Due to being so "responsible" at work, I completely overwhelmed and tired myself out. I kept running in circles trying to get away from the ever present negative emotions. Every time I thought I got away, I would eventually find myself staring back at myself in the mirror. It didn't matter if I changed where I lived, careers, relationships, or (wishfully thinking) family members.

I always circled back to where I started. I once again chose the same path. Was this some sick twist of the universe? I felt like I was in one of those damn fun houses that weren't so fun.

Have you ever been to a funeral where the deceased didn't know he was dead? I can guarantee at the time of the situation, I didn't want to have anything to do with what was transpiring. As the story unfolds, you will understand a bit of my awareness and how a fake sense of calm had brought great peace to the individual's mother.

I had worked side-by-side and sometimes car pooled with a woman, whom I will call Anna, for about 12 years. I had met a couple of her children who were close to my age. I also knew her son Dale who was one year younger than me from middle school. Anna's second husband Ron was critically ill in the hospital. I wasn't surprised when I got a phone call from a co-worker saying, "I have bad news about Anna." We were a tight knit group at work.

What shocked me was that it wasn't in regards to her husband. I was told that her son Dale had died the day before.

I had to have my co-worker repeat the devastating news because I couldn't comprehend it. The family went on a picnic to take a break from the stress of Ron being so sick. Dale had picked up a can of cola that he was drinking not knowing that a wasp had flow inside. He got stung several times in the mouth and tongue. No one knew that he was allergic to the stings. No one knew what was happening when they saw him loose the ability to breathe. Dale didn't know that he had died that day.

A few days later, our department at work shut down so that we could all attend the funeral. As the service commenced, I started to feel this strange energy swirling around the room. The franticness of the swirling rapidly increased. I then could feel/hear a voice say, "What's going on? What is everyone one doing here?" This panicked voice kept getting stronger. It took every ounce of energy to not get up and leave the church.

Everyone was under enough stress as it was. If I had gone running scared out of the building who knows what sort of chaos I would have created.

The service finally ended, and we filed down to the basement for lunch. As I sat there trying to act normal and choke down the Jell-O, Anna approached me and said, "Barb what is going on?" She had known that I sometimes had special awareness. I shook my head no and said nothing. That night, I got another dreaded phone call. Ron, Anna's husband died, around the time of the funeral. It was such a blow to us all.

Two days later, Anna came in to work to talk to me specifically (she was still on personal leave.) She marched up to me and said, "Barb, I'm asking you again. What is going on?" My intuition had let me know what I believed happened. I told her that:

    a. Ron had chosen to die because he needed to show Dale the way to the light.

    b. She was done loosing loved ones for the next years' time.

    c. Ron had left behind an unknown large life insurance policy.

    d. Care to share your folly?

She said, "Oh thank God. This all makes sense to me now. I had kept asking why Ron died." She gave me the warmest of hugs and then went home to grieve with a quieted mind. I'm in awe that Anna was able to sense that something amazing had transpired during her time of deep sorrow; that Ron's last role in life was to choose the path to help the ones he cared about.

The purpose of me writing this story was to not only get it out of my system but, more importantly, to be able to share what could be seen as a double tragedy into a story of awareness and love.

The Wounded Child

What small act of kindness left you feeling grateful the rest of your life?

I had to go into a same day clinic for minor surgery. My appointment was scheduled based on my mom's busy work schedule. We got to the clinic in plenty of time to prepare for the surgery. I had my vitals checked and was gowned up in the typical surgery attire. They had all of us patients stay with our families in the busy waiting room until it was our time. My mother kept busy by making calls on the complementary phone in the corner.

I sat there worrying about pain and scars. The nurse called my name and said it was time. I motioned to my mom that I was going in. She gave me a look of frustration and waved me away. The nurse was taken aback and said, "Don't you want to hug daughter?" She, too, got the same look of frustration and got waved away. The waiting room full of people went dead silent as:

   a. A stranger stood up and gave me a big hug assuring me everything was going to be all right.

b. The staff made the decision to delay the surgery due to not trusting the after care.
c. The nurse stomped on over and disconnected the phone my mother was using.
d. Care to share your folly?

There is a powerful surrendering technique that I have learned about after reading the book *Letting Go: The Pathway to Surrender* by David Hawkins.

I then completed several amazing surrendering training programs and meditations created by Michael Mackintosh. Both of these have allowed me to release negative stored emotions. I had, in many cases, been carrying most of them a good part of my life. The more I surrendered these emotions, the more feelings of freedom and joy have increased in my life.

There were different ways my subconscious let me know what I needed to surrender next. Reoccurring dreams was one way. Unexplained physical ailments would sometimes trigger awareness that another emotion was due to be released. I started to suffer from a swollen thyroid for the first time ever. My doctor caught it in its infancy during a routine exam. I was sent out for blood work and an ultrasound. Part of me knew that as the symptoms increased that this was an emotional issue.

I hunkered down with one of Michael's mediations that gently guided me each step of the way on how to determine where the pain was located in my body, where it stemmed from, how to release it, and turn it into joy.

I had used the same technique successfully before but as I was focusing on the discomfort of my swollen thyroid I started to get the sensation that I was being choked. Mild panic started to form at first as I followed the releasing technique. Plus, I was feeling a bit confused because in the past I was always able to determine what event in my life caused the pain.

The only memories that were surfacing were that I realized that as long as I could remember I couldn't stand the feeling of a tight scarf or shirt around my neck. I was able to successfully release the discomfort in my body both physically and emotionally. The question of what caused it still stumped me.

I called my mom and gave her a brief explanation of the surrendering and letting go work I was doing. I then asked her had there ever been a time that I had been choked as an infant. She said no although she could never stand the feeling of having anything tight around her neck. This was a surprise to me because I hadn't shared that I, too, had the same uncomfortable sensation. It wasn't until this occurrence that I truly believe that I inherited or somehow learned this emotion from my mother.

Upon deeper inner work and surrendering, I found that I was able to give love/positive energy but not receive it. This caused an unbalanced flow of energy. By healing my emotions, I can heal not only my physical body but my present life as well.

Nesting

Why are you hording that item?

I've heard of people suffering from empty nest syndrome. This is based more so on when one's children leave the house, and they are feeling the loss of energy.

I'm the opposite. I was suffering from full nest syndrome. I have lived in my condo for 7 seven years and accumulated all sorts of stuff that was doing nothing but taking up space. Not to mention all of the things I moved into the condo that I have vowed to get rid of and never did.

There were so many objects in my home that gave off unpleasant vibrations. Belongings and gifts from past relationships were tucked away in boxes covered with dust. I felt it was time to clear out the clutter.

With a new commitment to myself, I set aside an entire weekend to dig through every drawer, cupboard, box, closet, shelf, and everything else that was and wasn't moving. The first morning, I started at 3:30 a.m. I woke with the excitement to tackle it all. I started a pile for things to sell, another to donate, one for trash, and an "I have no idea what to do pile." I took everything out of the kitchen cupboards and cleaned each shelf along the way.

I kept my energy flowing by listening to CDs that I hadn't touched in years. If they didn't inspire me they, too, ended up in one of the piles. Some of the things I came across triggered a lot of unexpected memories and emotions. If an object gave off an unpleasant vibration, it automatically went into one of the piles regardless of the value. This included several pieces of furniture.

To my delight, I found a few unexpected or forgotten things. My favorite was a box of partially used Christmas cards. I immediately addressed one to my brother. A long time ago, it took him 4 or 5 years before he figured out I was sending him the same card every year. I had chosen this particular card because the front cover picture was of a group of people and animals fighting over an item on sale. At least, this was my interpretation of the picture.

The first couple of Christmases my brother would look at the card and say this picture doesn't make sense. It finally dawned on him that he was getting the exact same terrible card over and over. This has become a 23 year tradition.

I always look forward to his phone call of exasperation when he gets yet another one in the mail. I'm going to need to take the last card and see if I can legally have it copied so that the tradition is not broken.

We also have several gag gifts that have been swapped with family members for years. I've taken all of these horded items that were in storage and put them in the mail along with the card. A few other items I found during my intensive cleaning that took me by surprise were:

a. A man's thong that I swear I've never seen before.
b. A hidden stash of my previous boyfriend's Viagra.
c. A scratch off lottery ticket that won $100 but had expired several years before.
d. Care to share your folly?

I thought I was just about done with the cleaning when my PC hard drive crashed again. This particular PC had ongoing issues ever since the warranty ran out. I had replaced the drive twice already. There was a seemingly endless array of backups and transferred data files layered within its memory.

At first, I was pretty stressed out after realizing I lost about one week's worth of data (including several chapters of this book). All of those past pictures I was working on deleting, all of the letters of resignation, and all of the hopeful cover letters were gone.

The realization sunk in that I no longer had to search and decide what to do with all of the folders. I can't even begin to tell you how freeing this felt.

As my piles of sorted stuff left the condo, the feeling of freedom intensified. All of the unpleasant vibrations started to dissipate. It is amazing how much lighter my nest looks and feels. I've created a new sense of tranquility in my home.

Care to share a forgotten item that has resurfaced in your home during a deep cleaning binge?

Guilt

Ever feel you need to justify your innocence?

There were times in my life that I should have felt guilty. Like the constant playing of jokes on my dad's girlfriend. However, in most cases I felt guilt when there shouldn't have been any. There is one particular situation I carried for about 30 years. It wasn't until recently did I realize how much it still affected my life. I didn't know that the feelings can be easily released so I carried it like a long lost enemy. If I started to forget about it, the guilt would return to me in reoccurring bad dreams. It became a form of unintentional self-punishment.

We had a white bull terrier named Star. She was a lifelong playmate and always full of love. She would sit there patiently as us kids would climb all over her, wake her up, and I guess in some cases ate her dog food. (I'm still not convinced that my older sister poured milk and sugar over the dog food and fed it to me for breakfast.)

When I was 16, the dog had pretty much become deaf, blind, and arthritic. My mom loved that dog more than anything in the world. She couldn't face the fact that the dog was suffering and ignored the situation for a long time.

Me being the most responsible in the family packed the dog up and brought her to the veterinarian to have her put down. It was such a hard time because she was so happy to go for a ride in the car.

When we got to the clinic, she knew that something was wrong. Her joy from the car ride turned into fear. She started to shake and whine.

I had called the vet's office ahead of time so they were expecting us. All I remember is walking in, handing over the leash, and leaving. I had to be the one to bring her in because:

a. No one else in the family had a valid driver's license.
b. I was the only one the dog would trust to get in the car with.
c. Mom was away in treatment.
d. Care to share your folly?

At the time of this occurrence, my mom and dad were already divorced.

Dad lived about 30 miles away.

I'm not sure who told him about the dog but the subject was never mentioned until 32 years later.

My dad had a couple of small strokes which caused his memory to mostly go. On my frequent phone calls to him, we would usually laugh and talk about the same things over and over.

This usually pertained to the weather and what a wonderful life he had lived.

One day when I called, he was agitated.

Out of the blue, he told me he resented me for putting the dog down. This was within a few days of me working on releasing the guilt from my system.

My dad's resentment was like a slap in the face. I realized that for all of this time he carried these feelings for me. I took a deep breath and said, "Dad I was showing the dog mercy. She was so feeble and sick; she no longer was living a good life." My dad was astounded. It never occurred to him that the dog was old and lived a full life. He had thought I brought the dog in because I didn't want to be bothered any more.

For all of these years, Dad couldn't figure out why I didn't bring the dog to him so that he could take care of her.

Once this understanding had been reached between the two of us, I felt like a black cloud inside of my body was released. I'm not sure of how the mechanics worked, but I was not able to completely release the guilt until my dad forgave me. Since then our conversations have gone back to laughter.

Care to share a deep time of letting go of guilt?

Exploring

When was the last time you were up for a new adventure?

In the late '90s, I had a Canadian lover/travel companion. We spent time together traveling from adventure to adventure for a couple of wonderful years. We had met on a trip to Costa Rica and got together several times after.

He had a tremendous sense of humor that came out during the travels and while staying in contact via email. He started to create a story by writing a paragraph about our travels. Then he would send it to me to add the next paragraph.

I would add a twist to it and see what he came up with next. Together we created an amusing story. It was a great way to share and to get to know each other more.

I'm still a bit sad to think that the story was lost during one of my hard drive crashes.

We emailed pictures back and forth of ourselves and the surrounding community. One evening we had one of those rare blue moons.

I can still hear him laugh when I figured out how to use the timer on my camera. I dropped my drawers, took a picture of my full moon, and emailed it to the wrong email address.

You can imagine my mortification when the realization sunk in. This was way before any sort of sexting or similar activities had become popular. The term Living Hell may have been created thanks to me. The following transpired next:

a. The email provider sent me a notice of improper use and shut down my account.
b. My co-worker, who was the recipient of the email, became so uncomfortable after seeing the picture he quit his job.
c. The picture can still be found in Google images.
d. Care to share your folly?

To my knowledge, the self-taken picture was never confirmed to be me. I still chuckle at the thought of the evening I had hit send. I had felt so much shame, I wanted to crawl underneath my keyboard. It was years before I could admit to anyone what I had done. To you, it may appear to be no big deal. For me, I was simultaneously mortified and laughing at myself.

Your Doctor Said That?

I had worked for a laboratory for over 15 years for a company that required annual physicals. The company wanted to monitor us in case some of the things we were exposed to were hazardous to our health.

There were about 25 of us they would ship to a clinic over the period of one or two days. There were several exam rooms that were set aside just for us. Several different doctors would rotate to the room of the next available patient. While sitting there waiting in one of the exam rooms, I'm not sure who was more surprised when the doctor walked in.

We had previously met several years ago in Jamaica. It had been a wild week of partying. We both had been staying at a small hotel. All of the rooms had been booked by a group of friends with the exception of two rooms. In one were me and my roommate; in the other were the doctor and his wife. The four of us ended up hanging out together because the partying at the hotel sometimes got out of control.

After the vacation, we were not in contact until we crossed paths at the doctor's office. The last time I had seen him, we were doing lines of coke in the women's bathroom in a restaurant close to Ocho Rios. How did he handle the situation as he entered the room?

a. He asked if everything was irie.
b. He blushed and backed out the door mumbling about the wrong room.
c. He asked me if I knew where he could score any coke.
d. Care to share your folly?

This was the only time I ever tried using cocaine. I liked the way it made me feel and knew that I better stop while I still could. Perhaps it was the doctor's only time experimenting as well. I do have to admit I was surprised that someone with his education would not simply say no when it came to drugs. I feel very fortunate that I don't have an addictive personality. This one time experience could have lead down a long road of destruction.

Why Procreate?

Do you ever wonder why some people don't have the urge to have children?

I think I started to lose the calling at a young age. My mom liked to use me as a guinea pig. I was always the first one to try something new. This was encouraged by my mom and backed up by my siblings. Their theory was to send the youngest in first; if I survived, they would follow suit. Getting my ears pierced or jumping in the icy cold lake at the beginning of spring are good examples. My mother tried to convince me to get a tattoo at the age of 12.

At the time, she was into commercial real estate and was trying to sell a tattoo parlor. I have to admit for a brief period of time getting a turtle tattoo by my ankle had its appeal. I didn't know any kids in elementary school who had one. It would have almost been worth seeing how my grandfather would have reacted in the 1970s. In this case, I'm very grateful that I didn't succumb to her whims.

Unknown to me, I did become a part of a different type of whim. When I was in my early 20s, I was audited by the IRS. There was some initial confusion because they said I owed taxes on some property I had never heard of. I thought, *'How could I owe money on something I didn't own? There must be a mistake.'*

This was how I found out that my mother used my name and social security number in some sort of business transaction.

Who else could better steal your identity than your mother? She had gone bankrupt and needed a way to continue to earn money.

I'm not sure if she thought about the consequences it would have on me. I had called her and told her about being audited and my confusion. She started mumbling about some hidden deal.

That was when it dawned on me that she was involved. I never did get the whole story out of her. I did the following:

> a. I kept my mouth closed, paid the IRS, all the while debating on pressing charges.
> b. I completely denied knowing anything about the real estate transaction.
> c. I started collecting food stamps in her name to recuperate some of the losses.
> d. Care to share your folly?

Throughout the years, my mom continued to try to get me involved in her business practices.

I do admit my sister and I fell for her family partnership schemes. Mom was shrewd. She made money in the partnership while we ended up paying for both her taxes and ours. I feel her thoughts were if we lost money, it was our own fault for not completely understanding how the partnership worked.

There was a lot of painful truth to that. I learned never again to get involved in her dealings. More importantly, I learned that I could love and forgive her. The next time she needed money, I offered it to her in cash verses a contract.

When Was a Time Your Parent Got You Involved in an Unpleasant Situation?

My mother set me up with her drug dealer's younger brother. This all started when we stopped off at Joey's house so that my mom could pick something up. I believe I was 13 at the time.

I waited in the car while my mom ran inside. A good looking man of about 18 years old exited the house while I waited. I made some off handed comment about him when my mom returned. I'm not really sure of the motivation behind the act, but my mom decided that she and Joey would set us up. Most likely, my comment had something to do with it. I very rarely expressed interest in the opposite sex.

They arranged a plan to pick up the younger brother and bring him with us to my mom's night club. The thoughts were we would watch the band together then bring him home after.

I was feeling a bit nervous and didn't really know what to expect. There was confusion on my part as we arrived to pick up the younger brother. The man who emerged from the house to join us was not the same one I had seen the other day. Mom and I kept our mouths shut and brought the true younger brother with us.

Things weren't going the best to begin with when the night took a turn for the worse. This is what had happened later that evening:

a. We all got arrested for drug possession, but my charges were dropped because I was a minor.
b. The younger brother got drunk, left with a strange woman, and disappeared for a couple of days. This included a missing persons report.
c. I was sexually assaulted on the date in my mom's car.
d. Care to share your folly?

I never did figure out who the good looking man was I saw that day sitting in my mom's car. The whole episode left a lasting impression on me because I had blamed the misfortune on my mom for a long time. I had first stuffed the emotions down. When they started to surface I thought, *'What in the hell was she thinking? Aren't mothers supposed to keep their children free from harm?'*

I resented her for many years. I got tired of the nauseous feelings I got every time I thought about it. I had to really open my eyes and realize that she was trying to help me by setting me up with the man. There was no malicious intent that evening, things just happened to unravel out of control.

Funerals

When did a small stiffened laugh take on life of its own and get out of control?

As an adult, have you ever gotten the giggles in the middle of your sweet grandmother's funeral? In this case, I was in a Catholic church. It was a typical service with singing, standing, kneeling, and praying. The long service started to drag on. I didn't want to think about my grandma being gone, so I stopped paying attention to the words that were being spoken and tuned into my surroundings.

That was a mistake because I picked up on something very funny. I tried to cough away a few premature giggles. The harder I tried to suppress them, the harder I laughed. It didn't help that my sister sitting close to me was crying heavily. She gave me a surprised look because she thought I was sobbing.

By then the tears of laughter were seeping through my fingers that were covering my face. My brother assessed my actions accurately and decided it was a good time to discretely try and tickle me. The original cause of the giggles was:

a. The incense in the catholic mass was starting to smoke us all out.
b. A kamikaze fly was dive bombing my sister's face.
c. It turns out that the priest was the man with whom my aunt was having an affair.
d. Care to share your folly?

Grandma loved us children unconditionally. I will always think of her with fondness and love. I feel that her parting gift to us was creating one last chance to make us laugh. I know that somehow she was able to arrange the funny situation. It was her way of helping us through her funeral.

She was able to bring simple magic into our lives by taking something benign as a homemade pancake and turning it into the shape of a rabbit or a frog. She would picture the animal she was creating while she poured the batter. She would tell us how it looked. When the pancake arrived steaming hot on our plate we, too, could see the newly created animal.

When I grew older, I got distracted with my own life. I sometimes unintentionally "forgot" about her. It didn't matter how long I stayed out of touch. The next time I visited her, she was always so happy and appreciative to see me.

It wasn't until her time was almost at an end when I realized how deeply intelligent she was. I began to realize that most of her statements had two meanings. I had only focused on the simple obvious version. From her, I have a deeper understanding that what is being said isn't always what we hear. Every time I think of her loving ways, I feel deep gratitude for her open heart.

What Precious Story Can You Write Before it Gets Lost?

I had the honor to be a pall bearer for my beloved grandfather. It was in the middle of winter and not too many people were able to attend due to weather conditions.

When the ceremony concluded, I was placed at the front of the procession. It was my duty to guide the casket from the front of the church as it sat on top of a cart with wheels.

All went well as we wheeled the casket down the center aisle to the rear of the church. We made it through the double door exit without any issues. Once we were where outside, we were to lift the casket up and carry it down about 6 wide spaced stairs. The hearse was a short carrying distance away. No one warned me that:

   a. The stairs were covered in ice and we all went sliding down, casket and all.
   b. The contents (grandpa's body) shifted and ended up causing me to almost drop the unexpected extra weight.

c. There was already a casket in the hearse, and there was no room for grandpa.

d. Care to share your folly?

Grandpa's personality was a lot more reserved than grandma's.

When he was in his early 90s, my sister brought both grandparents into her home. She quit her job and administered home care.

We used to sneak into Grandpa's room at night to watch him while he was sleeping. He had caught a chill in his bones that he couldn't get rid of. He would wear his stocking cap pulled down tightly around his head to bed. He would burrow under mounds of blankets. The only things peeking out would be his eyes, nose, and mouth. He looked so cute all wrapped up while his creased cheeks sunk in. His dentures sat in a glass next to the bed. He didn't want to be seen without them.

Shortly after our sneaking glimpses of him, he fell terminally ill and was brought to the hospital. Grandpa knew his time on earth would be ending soon. He called us all to his room to say his final goodbyes.

He had already resigned to the fact he was leaving. His mind started to revert back to his younger years. He forgot who we were and started talking about working on the family farm.

To the mortification of my brother and my utter amusement Grandpa came up with a priceless tidbit. He told my brother to go to 7 corners in St. Paul and ask for Miss Ruby. He nudged by brother and simultaneously said, "For 2 bits, you know" nudge, nudge. Some people might be traumatized in discovering their grandfather indulged in promiscuity.

In my eyes, he finally started to show a bit of his adventurous side. I wish I had the sense to ask more questions about his past while he was still alive. I'm now quick certain that many fine stories came to their final end the day Grandpa died.

Out in the Cold

What new sense of freedom have you created for yourself?

I lived the majority of my life in Minnesota. Most of my life experiences took place there.

As part of my divorce, I kept the snow blower that my father had purchased for us as a Christmas gift. The monster of a machine had 5 speeds in forward and a couple in reverse. It was so large, I could barely see over the top of it.

I had been avoiding the snow blower for several snow falls. One day, the snow came down too fast and heavy to be easily shoveled.

I added gas to the blower and checked the oil level. I started to consult the manual in the driveway as I stood in 10 inches of heavy wet snow. There were levers and switches for turning on the gas, the electric starter, the clutch, the augur, the direction and angle of the snow throwing shoot, and the light.

There were so many new things to think about all at once. I set my mind knowing that I could get this baby to work.

I got her started and pulled every level and switch I could get my hands on.

The snow blower lurched forward at a rapid speed. The tires dug in and the machine started to eat away a path. I adjusted one more level before I threw that heavy wet snow high up into the air. It shot across the driveway and plastered a beautiful arch of wet snow across my neighbor's second story bedroom windows.

He happened to pull into his driveway just in time to witness the entire production. By the time he got out of truck, I was laughing so hard I had tears running down my face. Once I could get myself under control this was said:

a. You better wipe those tears off of your face before they freeze.
b. From now on, I'll do all the snow blowing for you (did I say this or my neighbor?)
c. I'm really sorry. I'll pay for any broken windows or any other damage I may have caused.
d. Care to share your folly?

Learning how to use a piece of machinery I've never used before and causing the snow to soar across the driveway left me with a sense of freedom. I needed the humorous release to know that everything was going to be fine. It didn't matter to me that my neighbor ending up thinking I was odd. On a different note, he was real quick to jump in and take over anytime he saw me with a power tool.

Roommates

When was a time that you let greed get in the way of your intuition?

Just about everyone I know has had trying situations with roommates.

Some of the situations were simple like the time I caught one peeing in the laundry tub because the bathroom was occupied. Then there was the time I found out another male roommate was going through my underwear drawer.

The least he could have done was refold the panties when he was done! I still get the willies thinking about it. I pulled the whole drawer out of the dresser and dumped its entirety into the washing machine. Shortly after, I told him it was time to leave.

The best, or should I say, the most upsetting roommate story was when I allowed a man named Jon to move in.

I had owned a split level home that had a walkout basement that wasn't being used. The basement consisted of an "L" shaped family room, laundry room, and a bathroom with a shower. I periodically would rent this area out when someone needed a place to stay.

I had been working as a restaurant manager at the time and was in the process of switching to a different one of the chain's locations.

One of my wait staff needed a place to live. Jon was a hard worker, well liked, and had just started classes at the University.

I was hesitant in letting him move in. However, he won me over by stating he could do some minor repairs on my house. When he first moved in, things went as planned. We had different schedules, and our paths rarely crossed.

The problems began late at night. He started having guests visit, some of which I knew. Then the visitors came I didn't know. He was going out to the bars, getting drunk, and bringing strange men home. This didn't fly with me because they had access to the rest of the house where I was trying to sleep. I laid there awake several times worried that these strangers might start to explore the house.

Jon would have them spend one night then dump them. In a couple of cases, these unknown men would call on the phone either somewhat embarrassed or demanding to speak to Jon. In one case, one showed up very angry at the front door asking where he was and who was I.

It turns out that Jon was stealing their credit cards while they stayed the night. He would then use the card to go on a shopping spree.

He mainly focused on married men knowing that they wouldn't press charges or else their wives may find out about their extracurricular activities. Many other bad incidents rapidly evolved. I asked him to leave immediately. I quickly changed the locks on the doors. I heard soon after that:

a. He tried stealing a credit card from a policeman.
b. His name wasn't Jon and that he was living, going to school, and bought a truck all under some guy's name who he had picked up in a bar.
c. He became a well-known Politician.
d. Care to share your folly?

I should have used my intuition when I felt hesitant in letting Jon move in.

The idea of collecting some extra cash and getting a few projects around the house completed clouded my discernment.

I was set to leave for Germany to visit a friend at the time I was kicking him out of my house. I debated on canceling my plans. Instead, I quickly put my bank and Credit Card Company on alert.

I asked my neighbors to watch my home for me while I was gone. They had the phone number of the place I was staying in case of an emergency.

I had heard through the grape vine that he had a female partner in crime. I have no idea if there was any truth to it. He did have access to my bank statements and account numbers while he lived with me. It did leave me on edge while I was out of the country.

Fortunately, nothing else transpired while I was away. He was the last roommate that I took in. I realized that my peace and harmony were more important to me than earning a few extra dollars.

Not Today

Remember a time when an unexpected person went out of their way to help you?

I bought my first car and a set of keys for $50 when I was sixteen.

No title existed nor did my driver's license. I called it my Chevy way-gone. It was a nondescript, tan-colored station wagon with fake wood side panels. She had bald tires and had one of those bench type seats in the rear that faced backwards. Not only did it give me a sense of freedom, I could pack about 9 of my friends into it. It guzzled the gas, usually started, and gave us the means to get to the parties in the warehouse district of St. Paul.

I kept it parked about one block away from where I lived so that my mom didn't see it. She didn't know if I had taken my driver's test. We weren't really talking to each other at that point in my life. She knew I was skipping school to work, but it was much easier for the two of us just to ignore each other than to converse.

One day, as I accidentally drove past her she looked up and gave me a look of comprehension. My ownership of the car soon came to an end when:

a. She called and had it towed.
b. She donated it to charity.
c. She took it for her own use because her car broke down.
d. Care to share your folly?

Soon after losing the car, I was able to obtain a driver license and drive legally. I'm very fortunate because one of my friend's moms, Pam, posed as my own and took me in for the driver's test. I had already done the class work the year before.

I passed the physical testing on the first try. It all went pretty smoothly until Pam was going to sign my mom's name.

She wasn't sure of the spelling. After a brief moment of mutual panic, she picked up the pen and made an impressive scribble.

Pam had been taking me for a few test drives prior to the test. She felt it was better for her to impersonate my mother than to have me drive illegally. Looking back, I feel so touched knowing how she put herself at risk to help me. I will always be grateful for her compassion. I paid $250 for my next car. I called her my Glad to Nova. She came along legally.

Being Ourselves

Do you dread family gatherings?

My brother, my sister, and I developed our own style of humor. It was a way to communicate with each other without talking about our feelings. It was a way to release tension and in our own way let the others know we cared. I always take great delight when I meet others whose humor fits into our style.

It was only when I looked at one of my siblings' dead pan faces that I knew something was brewing. We perfected this look of nonchalance as we became young adults. Our favorite time to use it was at family gatherings. It was best when there were one or two guests. We had an unwritten pact that the guest(s) would not be clued in as to what may transpire during our gathering.

Everyone would be holding a typical dinner conversation while at least one of us kids would be swapping out food items on other people's plate. The guest would look down at their plate in confusion. Where once their roll sat a full stick of butter would be in its place.

In some cases, food items would appear that weren't part of the planned dinner. For example, a banana would appear on a plate of spaghetti. One of us would engage the guest in conversation while the other was sneaking food items around or under the table then strategically place them on the unexpecting person's plate.

These actions pissed off by Dad's girlfriend Ruth to no end when she became the receiver of unwanted items. Ruth was an actress and singer who was used to being the center of attention but not of this kind. When food items got swapped on her plate, the drama would begin.

All of us, including my dad, would ignore her. She would start raising her voice and start making comments about how awful we kids were. All of which got purposely ignored which frustrated her even more.

Ruth's breaking point was when she ended up with a baked potato on her plate after she clearly stated she didn't want one. While Dad was engaged in conversation at the opposite end of the table she:

    a. Made up a little song about the potato and sang it loudly.

    b. Dumped it into my brother's water glass.

    c. Picked up the baked potato and threw it at my dad, smacking him in the middle of the forehead with it.

    d. Care to share your folly?

Her bold action took us all by surprise. She finally figured out that the best approach was either get beat or join us in our silliness. It must have been tough on her because here were three adult children seemly acting out of control in her eyes. It wasn't our intention to make the dinner guests uncomfortable.

Looking back I realize this was our way of sharing our sense of humor and camaraderie.

It Sounded Like a Good Idea at the Time

Tell me about your ingenuity.

It was an interesting experience writing this chapter. I thought it was going to be the most fun one of them all. I had created notes and a rough draft in my journal. I then sat down and starting typing the next draft on my PC.

I found myself exaggerating one of the stories listed below. I thought, *'This will be a lot more entertaining for the readers.'* The more I typed, the more de-energized I became.

I turn off the computer and crawled into bed early. A few hours later, I woke up feeling depressed. I rationalized it as digging into my past and stirring up stored emotions.

The next morning, as I was doing my daily practice of journaling, an explanation came to me. I'm writing this book to help you let go of your past resentment.

What is the point if I'm not being truthful? Wouldn't it be much better if it all of the information came from the heart? In one simple swoop, I corrected the story and the depressed feeling quickly diminished. My feeling of excitement rapidly returned.

While growing up, we lived on a lake for a short period of time.

Our house was situated on a shallow bay with about eight other homes. The water was very murky, and the bottom was covered in sludge.

We spent most of the summer playing in the water and fishing. Toward the end of the summer, we started to get bored.

My brother and I spent days digging a drop off straight out from our dock. I thought everyone would marvel at our ingenuity in getting the hole so deep.

We stood there straight faced as our dad went on a leisurely walk in waste deep water. Our breaths were held as he took that last crucial step. He completely disappeared below the surface with hardly a ripple.

A few excruciating moments later dad resurfaced ready to kill. His hair was hanging down on one side of his head. He wore his hair in a comb over fashion that was supposed to hide his bald dome. As he started to look around angry and a bit bewildered, we jumped into action and:

    a. Started mumbling about those damn neighbors.
    b. My brother started to dive for my dad's glasses.

c. I tried to comb dad's hair back over the top of his head with my fingers.

d. Care to share your folly?

After my dad started to cool down from his unexpected plunge, he started to ask questions. He couldn't believe we got the hole so deep. We found someone to marvel at our ingenuity. We had dug the hole with the thought of catching one of our neighborhood friends. We never dreamt it would be our dad who fell into the trap. Upon reflection, I realized this was on a turning point in our lives. We were at a time where dad starting showing interest in our projects.

Where is a Place That You Have Always Felt Safe?

I was between 12 – 15 years old in the early 80's. My mother owned a large live music club. It drew in a wide variety of people due to its touristic location and the diversity of the live music. It was located in a picturesque town along a major river. During the summer, the Harleys would be stretched up and down the block.

On the weekends, my brother and I would do various jobs depending on the need and our age constraints. In most cases, I was the cashier for the cover charge. I would sit in a small booth near the front door with my till. I would collect the money and stamp the back of people's hands so that people could come and go as they pleased. There was a chalk board on the front of the booth that listed the band and the cover charge amount.

One Sunday evening, business started out slow. Out of boredom, I added a statement to the bottom of the chalk board – All weapons must be checked.

To my and the bouncer's astonishment, a gun was removed from an ankle strap and gently laid into my hands. Later on, a set of brass knuckles were handed over. I carefully place the two items next to me. My mom came to the front door to collect the extra cash so that it wouldn't get stolen – go figure. What happened when she got to the booth?

a. She looked at the sign and told me to erase the "All weapons must be checked" statement because it might dissuade people with weapons to come to the club.

b. She didn't notice anything amiss including when I had to remove the brass knuckles from the till to get at the $20s.

c. She became instantly concerned because there wasn't enough money collected yet to pay the band's wages.

d. Care to share your folly?

I will always look back fondly at my mom's club that had gone bankrupt. I was exposed at an impressionable age to a large variety of live music, lasting job skills, and a very strong sense of community. Depending on the type of music or the time of day, the patrons greatly varied. It gave me the opportunity to meet a plethora of interesting characters; some of them with weapons but most without. I took great comfort while writing this story. I realized that I had always felt safe in that environment. I will always consider the bar to be one of my past secure homes.

The Manipulation Game

How do you feel when you are being manipulated?

While I was conducting the deep cleaning of my condo, I came across pictures of some of my past boyfriends. As I threw the pictures in the trash, I started to acknowledge a common trait in all of them that I had never noticed before.

I had known that there were times some of their actions puzzled me. These actions made me feel defensive and uneasy. I never thought to dig deeper into the situation. I only knew I was annoyed but didn't understand why.

The best way I can explain it is by giving you an example of one of the most recent triggers. I had a conversation with a man with whom I was no longer involved. He made sure to tell me for about the 6th time how his daughter wanted to marry a man just like him, then he would pause and wait for me to agree with his daughter's desires.

The message I got from him was she could see how wonderful he was but why couldn't I? It always left me feeling like I should say something I didn't feel; that I was a bad person for not agreeing and making him feel better about himself.

I did feel some compassion for him but more so felt the irony of him still being married, and he was cheating on his wife. Even though he didn't say it directly, it sounded to me like his daughter wanted to marry a deceiving man just like him.

I couldn't figure out why he kept pushing the subject. It finally dawned on me that he was trying to manipulate me.

This really rubbed me the wrong way. I hated this type of game playing. My mom did it to me my whole life. Wait a minute I just said my mom played the manipulation game on me my whole life!?! I sat there a bit stunned, waiting for the next surprise to surface. Up it came like a bad gas bubble. I, too, had been playing these types of games my whole life.

Even though boyfriends had tried to me tell how I made them feel uncomfortable at times, I blew it off as it being their fault. Talk about the law of attraction kicking in. Only these were very appalling laws I was attracting.

I was such a pro at the playing the manipulation game, I didn't even realize that I was doing it. I was able to cast guilt and shame like a pair of dice. I even got one of my boyfriends to do a few things he didn't want to. We both felt terrible after. I'm now able to laugh about it and hope he can, too. One of those things was:

a. Talking him into getting a mullet.
b. Get matching tattoos.

c. Going on a formal cruise and wearing a tux.
d. Care to share your folly?

The whole realization of uncovering this trait had brought an immediate sense of relief. Deep down, I knew there was sometime wrong, but I didn't know what it was. I'm not proud of my actions but am enlightened that I was able to truly see myself. Now I'm excited to move forward without the heavy weight of manipulation in the pit of my stomach.

It Wasn't My Time to Die

Ever wonder why you haven't been pulled off of the planet?

Most of us have heard that our time to die is predestined. Whether this is true or not, I can't say. Apparently, the day I blew up the gas oven wasn't my time to leave the planet. If I had, I do believe I would have won one of the Darwin awards.

When I was about 17, my friend Irene lived on the third floor of an old house that was turned into apartments. Due to the poor air flow of her unit that used to be an attic, it was usually in the upper 80s in the middle of the Minnesota winter. The kitchen and living room windows were left open a few inches for ventilation. The tropical feeling of the hot air, inspired us to perfect our rum and fruit blender drinks.

After our second or third batch of drinks, we decided to throw some nachos in the oven. I turned the knob on the front of the oven to start preheating. The gas burners inside the oven didn't ignite. The cross breeze from the open windows had blown the pilot light out. I turned the knob back to off as we searched for matches.

What I hadn't noticed was that I had turned the outer plastic part of the knob to off while the inner metal knob had stayed frozen to the on position. The open window breeze effectively sucked the gas smell outside. There was no hint of it as I struck the match.

All I remember was the beautiful blue flames shooting past my head and getting thrown backwards off my feet. The explosion was strong enough to blow the curtains and pictures off of the wall and dislodge the entire range. I don't understand the science behind it but fortunately the fire appeared to be extinguished after the blast.

It was then that I was able to smell the gas leaking out of the ruptured pipe coming out of the wall. We quickly grabbed our jackets and went running out of the house yelling gas leak! The neighbors in the old house all quickly filed out. The house next door dialed 911.

We all hurdled together in the cold Minnesota winter air while waiting for the gas company to arrive. It was then that Irene noticed that:

    a. Her apartment was on fire.
    b. All of the snow had been melted off of the roof and was creating dangerously sharp icicles off of the gutters.
    c. My bangs, eyebrows, and eye lashes were missing.
    d. Care to share your folly?

This could have been a very serious situation. I only sustained a few minor injuries.

If I was a cat, I would have lost one of my nine lives that evening. Irene had witnessed the explosion and couldn't believe I walked away or should I say ran away from the kitchen. I like to believe there are many reasons why I didn't leave the planet that evening. I'm not sure if I had a protective shield around me at the time or if I was spared to help others. I do know that I'm very grateful to be sitting here writing this book.

Memorial Day Weekend

What sort of magical moment do you remember as a child?

Most of my memories of Memorial Day in Minnesota were wet ones. On one particular Memorial Day, the rain caused the traditional holiday picnic to be soggy and somewhat cold.

This didn't deter me and my lifelong friend Irene from bundling up with the thoughts of spending the day outdoors.

We packed a picnic basket, a large bottle of wine, and a blanket. We tramped off to Como Park to eat, drink, and feed the chipmunks.

It was drizzling out. Our blanket started to get muddy and our hair and cloths were becoming saturated. The novelty of sitting in the periodic sputters of rain started to diminish. The chipmunks weren't even out playing. We packed our remaining food and empty bottle of wine in the car and headed to the zoo area of the park.

In the zoo, there was a circular shaped display for seals. The center of the display had rock type ledges on which the seals could sit. Surrounding these ledges was water where the seals would swim and beg for food. Next to the enclosure, there was a small stand where you could purchase a cone of seal food. The package consisted of cold smelly headless fish.

We each bought our own package and brought it back to the seal enclosure. The seals were used to watching the people and knew who had the food. They would line up in front of us in the water barking for the fish.

I wasn't overly excited to touch the headless fish because they had a layer of slime on them. I used my fingernails to pinch the tails and flick the dead fish to the eager seals. Directly in front of me was a large boisterous seal. He was fast and pretty much swam on top of the other seals to get to the fish first. To the left of us were two small boys hanging over the edge of the railing for a better view.

The wind started to pick up as did the rain.

I had one exceptionally slimy fish left. I wanted to give it to a small seal that was looking hopefully at the two small boys. As I started to flick the last fish, it stuck to my fingernail. I gave my hand a forceful shake and launched it into the air.

The fish landed on the back of the neck of one of the small boys as he leaned over the side of the railing. He reached back and grabbed the fish from his neck. At first he looked shocked then terror set in. Right before he started to wail his mom said:

    a. Oh look Mickey! You still have a fish left.
    b. I told you to quit playing with your food.
    c. Were you trying to sneak the fish home with you again?
    d. Care to share your folly?

I wanted to walk over and explain the bad throw episode, but I was laughing so hard I couldn't move. The little boy was becoming more hysterical.

My friend started to push me out of the area before I caused even more of a commotion.

I looked back shortly after. I saw the mother was comforting the sobbing boy. He was starting to calm down a bit. He was looking up into the rain with a puzzled look on his face. Did he think the fish came in the rain? I hate to think how the term raining cats and dogs came about.

I had questioned my decision to leave the scene verses staying and explaining what had happened. If I had been in the boy's shoes, I believe I would have liked to say in the sense of wonder over the event. Perhaps I sparked a form of magic in his life that otherwise would not have otherwise transpired.

Why Is The Book Called Resentment: How to Let Go of Bitterness in an Entertaining Way?

a. The idea came to me in a dream.
b. It's a metaphor for letting go of the blues from the past.
c. The title is so catchy that it is hard to resist checking it out.
d. Care to share your folly?

Dancing in Your Groove

With a great sense of gratitude and release, I'm finishing this book. I tried to capture a diversity of stories for you to enjoy and contemplate.

Now it is your time to get out of your rut and into your groove. Can you see the absurdity, humor, or hurt from past events? On a different level, start to uncover a deeper meaning as you look at those occurrences in a new light. Sit down with you journal. Knock off your story. Don't ever lose the knowing that you are a beautiful person. Forgive those who intentionally or unintentionally caused you hurt. Share your story, follies, and wisdom with the rest of us. Feel the sense of freedom you achieve by letting go of your old baggage.

Now it is your chance to find the Gold at the End of YOUR Rainbow.

Join the Journey Online Today – it's FREE

Now it's your turn to share your experiences in a safe place. Create your own liberating story where you will be heard and valued. A place where you can grow and let go of past resentment. I admire your brilliance and look forward to reading all that you have to share.

By caring to share, we can appreciate the inner beauty within all of us and have a few good laughs and cries along the way. Try dancing with the ideas and see what surfaces. Join in on the excitement and visit www.barbbailey.com to choose the correct outcome for each story and pick your overcoming resentment free gift package. Here you will find the link to joining The Blue Rainbow Community on Facebook as well.

The more we support each other, the more we can grow and move on. Your story is important. Your life is important. Come to a safe space where you can share and let go.

I'll see you there.

Many smiles and love.

Barb

P.S.

Kindly note: by sharing your stories we can all grow and learn together. By simply venting a situation, it not only aggravates the situation, it can bring others down as well. Does your story bring you a sense of freedom? A deep meaning? Or does it only leave you feeling angry? Until you can find the positive note in it, you most likely will not achieve the letting go sensation.

The Great Vibrations Don't Stop Here!

Here are a few more kindle, paperback and audio books you will benefit from:

How to Detach from Negative People While Maintaining a Positive Attitude

Remote Energy: How to Send Healing Energy to Someone You Love.

How to Stop Being A Bitch by Being Truthful With Yourself

How to Heal Your Wounded Heart so You Can Love Freely

How to Write Off Guilt: Setting Free the Past through Journaling

Is there a particular subject you would like to learn about or have more understanding? Reach out and contact me. Not only am I available for personal mentoring, I'm very excited to create more books, training and meditations. Ask me how I can help you on your path of personal growth.

My stories start here:

By letting go of my resentment and bitterness, I've opened the door to light at the end of the blue rainbow.

Printed in Great Britain
by Amazon

30429364R00074